I Was the One I Was Waiting For

From Anxious Attachment and Codependency to Radical Self-Love: A Memoir

Heather Wild

Heather on Health

© 2025 Heather on Health. All rights reserved.

Published by Heather on Health. Written under the pen name Heather Wild.

No part of this book may be reproduced, stored in a retrieval system, or transmitted in any form or by any means – electronic, mechanical, photocopying, recording, or otherwise – without the prior written permission of the publisher, except for brief quotations used in reviews or scholarly works.

This memoir is a work of nonfiction based on the author's personal experiences. Names and identifying details have been changed to protect privacy. The author has written this book to the best of her recollection.

Cover photo by Angela Speller at Velvet Boudoir. All rights reserved.

For permissions, contact: info@heateronhealth.com

Heather Dolson (Heather Wild)

Contents

Why I Wrote This Book — 1

1. Jake: The First Cut is the Deepest — 4
   Not Being Chosen
2. Ezra — 9
   Where the Music Led Me
3. Nora — 14
   The Fire Between Us
4. Tal — 20
   You Can't Ask a Man to Run Without Legs
5. David: The White Night Myth — 26
   Red Flags and Red Dresses
6. My Brief Time as a Wife — 32
   Be Seen and Not Heard
7. Rory Grace — 37
   Coming Home, Starting Over
8. Sam's Story — 41
   When Stability Shows Up
9. What My Body Always Knew — 46
   The Lesson of Eddie

10.	Eddie and the Echoes Unraveling the Urge to Check	54
11.	Craving Proof	58
12.	Speaking the Standard	68
13.	Outgrowing the Loop When Emotional Intimacy Isn't Enough	71
14.	Attunement	74
15.	My True Freedom Returning to Me Again and Again	77
Letter to the Reader		86
A Note to Readers		87
Stay Connected		88
About the Author		90

Why I Wrote This Book

It was a trusted friend who first suggested I write my story—that it might be cathartic. That was two years ago. I sat down and wrote a little, but I didn't fully dive in. I planted the seed.

Now, two years later, I'm ready.

I thought: *What if I could revise as I write... purge as I integrate... fold every version of my past self into the wholeness I now claim?*

Yum. That felt right.

For years, my fatal flaw in relationships was trying to "fix" the men I loved. I entered situationships as the mother, the healer, the rescuer—hoping, naively, *maybe this one will change for me.*

But that impulse was never love.

It was insecurity.

It was unworthiness dressed up as caretaking.

I see that now.

I repeated these stories in my mind:

- *It's hard to be with me.*

- *I'm a single mom. A partner can't handle my reality.*
- *I don't have time to date.*
- *I'll never remarry.*
- *No man could live with us—it'd be too hard on the kids.*
- *Blended families? That sounds like a mess.*

So I lived that story—the struggling single mom who was hard to love.

This shift began when I stumbled into a Neville Goddard Facebook group. I found a thriving community and a compassionate mentor who broke down Neville's teachings in a way I could truly understand. It changed me forever.

I started to remember the truth of who I am. I remembered that ***I AM* is the one true cause**. And if that's true—then I could change the story. I could revise what I was imagining. I could even revise the past.—not to undo it, but to soften its hold. To feel into the love, healing, and wholeness that belong to me now.

This book is part memoir, part love letter to the lessons I've learned. Writing it has been cathartic—like alchemy. A way to transmute heartbreak into wisdom. All names have been changed, and as I wrote, I revised.

Neville teaches: "Change your conception of yourself and you will automatically change the world in which you live."

Revision is forgiveness.

Revision is freedom.

Why I'm Sharing My Story

I'm tired of silencing myself. Because my story lives in my body—still screaming to be heard. Because I spent years waiting to be chosen, saved, or rescued—only to realize **I was the one I was waiting for**.

I wrote this book for the women who keep loving harder, hoping it will suffice. For the mothers who thought their worth was measured by who they cared for. For anyone who's found themselves returning—even when every fiber of their body begged them not to.

I wrote it to give voice to what was never named: the shame, the patterns, the anxious ache. To unravel anxious attachment and codependency, and discover what was always there beneath it all: **me**.

I wrote it because healing doesn't have to be silent. We don't have to carry these stories alone. Maybe, in reading mine, you'll feel your own voice rising—softer, stronger, wilder.

You are the one you've been waiting for.

Jake: The First Cut is the Deepest

Not Being Chosen

I think it's time to start talking about my relationship history. I didn't want to overload my good friend with it because he was getting triggered. And yes, him and I need to take space sometimes from talking about our relationship troubles. I love him dearly, but sometimes it can be too much on each other, and we both start just looping around things. And I need to alchemize this in some way.

I've felt this book calling me from deep inside—the book that tells my love story, unfiltered. Not the fairy tale kind, but the kind that cracks you open. The kind that leaves wounds that still throb years later. The kind that teaches you about co-dependency, anxious attachment, and how much we mistake being wanted for being loved.

Maybe I need to voice it out, just like this. Speak it raw. Let it pour out before I try to make it pretty.

Today, I couldn't stop thinking about Jake. My first love. The place where it all began—or at least where I started to *notice* the patterns that would follow me for years. I was reflecting on my original relationship wound. This probably wasn't even the original one. I mean, you can go back to childhood and really dig deep into where it starts. But this was the first meaningful romantic relationship of my life at that point.

I met Jake when I was sixteen. He was sixteen too—just four months younger than me, but we were in different grades, different schools. We always laughed about that because I was the "older woman." From the beginning, he was my best friend. My first real love. We gave each other confidence. We were just kids, but it was real. And we made so many mistakes. I still tear up thinking about him.

We didn't have a clean breakup. It was messy and drawn-out, full of longing and unfinished business. I chose to leave. We were headed to different cities for university. I was eighteen and desperate to break free—from my hometown, the partying scene, and even from Jake, in a way. I knew I loved him, but I felt like I had to leave.

Looking back, I realize how much of that time was wrapped in alcohol, drugs, anxiety, and the craving to belong. I drank and smoked to escape. So did he. At that age, it felt normal. Now, I see the addiction in both of us. Looking back, I wish I would have done high school so differently. But of course, we say that so easily when we're older and more mature.

We drifted. Different cities, different lives. But we didn't let go. We still saw each other that first year of university, even though we weren't together. I dated other people. I'm sure he did too. Then I transferred to his city for my second year— Windsor—not for him, but because I was finished with where I was and I felt this deep urge to move on. Still, I won't pretend part of me wasn't hoping we'd reconnect. I think I had genuinely wanted to go to Windsor, but I was in such a rebellious mode when we graduated. I wanted to do something different, to get away from everybody that was going there. Everyone from my small town, Chatham, went there—or that's what I told myself.

And then I ended up there.

That same summer before the transfer, he was home. I was home. He had a girlfriend. And it broke my heart. And that same summer… we slept together.

I was the *other woman* when he had a girlfriend. That was my first experience of betrayal—being involved in it, feeling it twist inside me.

It was gut-wrenching. It was so empty. And yet I just wanted him so badly. I needed his love and his validation so badly. Even when it hurt.

When I moved to Windsor, I knew right away—he was seeing someone else. I could feel it in his energy. He still cared. He introduced me to friends, helped me settle in. But there was a wall. And I remember the moment he finally came over and said it.

I'll never forget what he said:

"I just want to put you in a box on the shelf for later."

That was the moment. The wound.

The first time I really felt *not chosen*. Not fully. Not enough.

And still, we didn't end it. We clung to each other for years. Back and forth. Hurting and healing and hurting again. We'd reconnect and then disappear. It was never clean. Never kind.

One time, years later, I had just moved to Toronto. He was there too. We reconnected. He was working at a pub, and my dad and I were there. Dad was helping me move my stuff. Jake pulled me into the back, lifted me on the counter and we had sex, like something out of a movie. And then—just like that—he disappeared again. I don't know what his situation was. I just know it shattered me.

A few days later, I ended up on the doorstep of Ezra. That's the next chapter. He was 52. I was 23. Another wound. Another lesson. Another reflection of what I thought I was worth.

But it started with Jake.

That first love taught me what it felt like to be wanted—but not fully held. To be almost chosen. To keep reaching for something that couldn't love me back in the way I needed.

He was more than a boyfriend. He was the beginning. The first one who made me feel beautiful, wanted, alive in my body. We gave each other confidence—but I gave away parts of myself I didn't yet understand.

And I kept reaching, for years.

Now, as I write this—older, wiser, still healing—I can see what I couldn't back then. I wasn't just chasing *Jake*. I was chasing proof that I was worthy. That I mattered. That I was enough.

And that ache didn't end with him. It only shapeshifted—into other men, other dynamics, other quiet betrayals that mirrored my own self-abandonment.

Ezra was the next mirror. On first appearances, he was everything Jake was not—steady, loyal, available. The contrast was jarring. And for a while, I thought maybe this was it—maybe safety could finally settle my longing. But even safety, without depth, can feel like a cage.

Ezra

Where the Music Led Me

I'm not sure if I believe in fate, but the way I met Ezra—it all just happened so beautifully.

First, I have to mention my best friend, Nora. I met her when I was 20, right in the thick of that heartbreak with Jake. I wasn't doing well—barely functioning in school, floundering through my third year of nursing. I had stopped going to class, smoking a lot of weed, and sinking into passive suicidal thoughts. I would soak in the bathtub and think, *If I died here, would anyone even know?*

At that time, I lived alone with my two kittens. It was a dark period, but I had a friend who cared deeply. He sat me down one day, looked me in the eye, and said, "You don't need antidepressants—it's situational. That stuff's just a Band-Aid." And I heard him. I believed him. I weaned myself off the meds and decided to change my situation. I listened to my soul.

I withdrew from nursing school, packed up the cats, and moved home to stay with my mom and dad. I knew I couldn't stay there long—I had to find my next step. Somehow, I ended up in Toronto at a yoga school. I didn't know much about yoga at the time, but something in me just knew—it was the answer.

That's where I met Nora. She's her own chapter, her own book, honestly. But for now, I'll just say we became very close. I stayed in Toronto for about two years, studying yoga and working at the school. Even after I moved back home to finish my nursing degree, Nora and I stayed connected—we'd visit and travel the distance to see each other.

One summer, Nora won tickets to a jazz festival and invited me to join her. It was at that Jazz Fest that I met him—Ezra.

We were on a bus being shuttled to different jazz clubs around the city. There he was—this older, attractive man with a camera around his neck. He was there as a photographer. He approached me—charming, persistent, romantic. He asked me to dance. There was chemistry, no question. We exchanged numbers.

Back then, things were different—we Skyped a few times, had some scattered conversations. I finished my degree, but I knew I wanted to go back to Toronto to start my nursing career. I let him know I was moving back, and he said, "Let me know when you're here."

Picking up the pieces after Jake, from stolen moments in the back room of that pub—feeling discarded and unchosen—I found myself on the doorstep of Ezra's place, guitar in hand.

And that's how it started.

We played music. We shared ourselves. Ezra was brilliant—he taught me almost everything I know on the guitar. I spent the next 3–4 years with him, in this back-and-forth rhythm. Just like with Jake, there was always this cycle of breaking up and getting back together. That pattern followed me into adulthood.

Ezra and I didn't live together at first. We each had our own places in Toronto, trying to make time between work and life. About a year and a half in, we decided to move in together—thinking it would solve everything: time, money, disconnection.

That's when I started to lose myself.

I'd never lived with a man before. I didn't know how to protect my space, my time, my identity. I began to feel left out when he'd go off and do things without me like band practice. By then, Nora and I had had a falling out—so I was also grieving her absence.

There was always this strange dynamic between Ezra and me—especially the age gap. I liked being different, standing out, but I also felt the duality of it. One time we were shopping, and a salesperson mistook him for my father. Ezra corrected him, saying, "Oh no—this is my love." But I was always aware. One of my good friends even shared her first impressions when she met us together for the first time, "What's this beautiful girl doing with this older man?"

Eventually, the codependency got heavier. The volatility, the arguing—it crept in. I started feeling deep down that there was no future here. I loved him, yes, but I was also waking up to something else.

I was starting to wonder if I wanted to become a mother. I was about 27 and working with an expressive arts therapist. Something was being uncovered—a desire I had long denied. I wanted to be a mom. I could feel it in my body. And I knew, deep down, it wouldn't be with Ezra.

He already had a child from a previous casual relationship. His son spent weekends with us. But when I brought up having children, he was honest—he was done. I remember him saying once, "I wish I was 10 or 15 years younger, baby." And I knew. I knew right then.

Our fights got worse. We were arguing about money. He wanted to take a trip, and I just couldn't afford it. I was working part-time and still immersed in my expressive art therapy program. I cried. I remember saying, "I don't have the money," and he snapped: "Would you stop your fucking crying?" That's just one moment—but it gives a window into how toxic it got.

Another time, during a fight, he had me pinned on the ground in our bedroom. I remember standing in the hallway, taking off my shoe, furious—thank God I threw it at the wall and not at him. It was chaos. And yet... there was passion. There was connection. Ezra was the man who helped me step into my womanhood. I embraced my natural beauty with him. But I was also deeply unhappy.

And I couldn't leave. I didn't know how. So instead—I cheated.

With Jake.

And it wrecked me. It was one of the worst things I've ever done. The guilt was unbearable. I thought, *I must be a masochist.* Eventually, I told Ezra. I had to. It was killing me.

We still had a trip to Cuba booked. He was angry, but he forgave me—or at least said he did. When his anger softened he told me, "I cheated in my twenties too honey." He got it. But even after the forgiveness, it simmered. It stayed between us.

In Cuba, we went to a club, and the local women were all over him—and every other foreign man. They were looking for a way out. It made me uncomfortable, especially seeing him enjoying the attention. One of the women came up to me and said, "I'll take care of your man tonight. Give you a break, sweetie." She wasn't trying to hurt me—she was just honest. She explained what it was like there. I felt empathy more than anything. But it shook me.

The final straw? One night, we were out at one of his work parties. He did special effects on film sets, and this was an industry event. I don't even remember what the fight was about, but I remember him calling me a bitch—right there, on the street in Toronto.

That was it.

I knew I had to leave. And in the letting go, he came to me and said, "Please don't go." We shared one last lovemaking session of tenderness. I had already moved into the spare room and was packing. I was on my way out.

And that night—after 4 years of withdrawal birth control method—he didn't.

Two weeks later, I was at my naturopath's office. I had been going there for natural treatment for cervical dysplasia. I casually mentioned, "I'm a bit late—it's probably stress. I've decided to leave the relationship that has been causing me stress." She suggested a pregnancy test.

A few minutes later, she came back in the room with her resident and said, "We have some news." They were both beaming and excited.

And that's when my entire world shifted.

I found out I was pregnant with my son.

And just like that, everything changed.

The ache of leaving Ezra, the uncertainty of what came next—none of it mattered in that moment. I was carrying life. And new life has a way of rerouting everything you thought you knew.

What came next wasn't just about relationships anymore. It was about motherhood. About identity. About becoming.

And that journey began with Nora.

Nora

♥

The Fire Between Us

I've been thinking about how friendships change as I evolve—how people fall away as I rise into deeper truths within myself. It made me think of Nora.

I remember the first time I met her. We were both in Toronto, at the yoga school, enrolled in the creative arts and drama intensive. The day she walked in, her energy filled the entire room. She was a force—big presence, edgy, intelligent, articulate, a little intimidating. I admired her instantly.

During one of our exercises, we had to dramatize scenes from someone's life. I was the one chosen. The theme we explored was attachment and detachment. We acted out childhood memories with my sister, and reflections from my first relationship with Jake. I was only twenty then, still naïve to so much I've lived through now.

At one point, the dramatization turned into improvisation. Nora was down on one knee in the center of the circle, playing a part, trying to win me over in a romantic way. I couldn't move towards her. Our teacher simply said, "That's not what gets her." It was such a real and beautiful moment—something about it etched into my memory forever.

After that, Nora and I started talking more after class. A slow blooming that turned fast. Soon, she became my ride-or-die friend. We spent so much time together—those were my drugs, sex, and rock and roll years, and some of my wildest experiences were with her by my side.

Not long after, I decided to leave Toronto to finish my nursing degree back home. By then, I had already left my position at the yoga school—it was a toxic environment, but that's another story for another book. I was unemployed, directionless, longing for something solid again. That's when my university called, urging me to come back before the program requirements changed. Perfect timing.

Even after I left, our friendship kept evolving. We were young, single, unattached—traveling back and forth between Toronto and Chatham, staying at each other's places, weaving our lives together with adventures and confessions.

Over time, our bond deepened. It was more than friendship. There was an attraction of souls, a mutual love and respect. I remember bringing Nora to a friend's wedding as my date without giving it a second thought. Later, my parents told me how they noticed the way she looked at me while I was dancing with someone else. It illuminated a dynamic I hadn't been willing to name.

We explored beyond friendship. Physical. Sexual. It was new to me, scary, but I had never felt closer to someone—more seen, more understood, more valued. I was in love with her. I would have done anything for her.

Shortly after that wedding, she called me upset. Her ex-boyfriend was being deported, and she felt the need to do something. Just like that, they got married. It broke my heart, but I didn't ever say that.

After all, we were undefined—just playing, exploring. I shifted into supportive friend mode, showing up for her in the way she needed. I even wrote a letter for their immigration case, testifying to their relationship.

That's how I got to know Samir.

At the time, I was still with Ezra, but I often spent time independently with Nora and Samir. I was seeing a therapist too, feeling the dissatisfaction in my relationship with Ezra, confused about my sexuality, seeking clarity. I remember sharing about Nora and Samir with my therapist. She just looked at me and said, "You're playing with fire."

That summed it up perfectly.

Because the love between Nora and I was still there. It only expanded into a triangle. I became a fantasy for Samir. They talked about bringing me into their marriage because the love and attraction ran so deep.

One night, we tried. I don't remember the details clearly—just the uncertainty, the excitement, the discomfort, the thrill of something new.

I don't think it went too far... until it did.

Boundaries were never spoken, but they were crossed. That night, alcohol was involved. Nora had gone to bed after an evening of drinking, dancing, and shenanigans. Samir stayed up with me in the living room. He had other plans. He acted on them. I was too drunk to stop him or say anything.

Nora walked out and saw it all.

Understandably, she was upset. She told me to leave. So there I was, in the middle of the night, heartbroken, crying as I waited for the bus in East Toronto to get to the subway. That was the end of us.

I grieved her deeply. Felt guilty for my part. "Playing with fire" finally made sense—I now had a story to prove it.

I never told Ezra the truth—only that Nora and I had a falling out. Shortly after, he and I moved in together. I felt her absence like a phantom limb.

After a year or so, though, Nora and I reunited. She thanked me. She told me I had been the catalyst for her to leave Samir. She hadn't been happy, and that night was the final straw.

Samir had reached out to me a couple times, so I knew they'd separated. Immigration was complete by then. But my loyalty was to Nora. I cut off contact with him. She and I healed, but we never revisited the sexual side of our relationship.

Nora stayed in my life through motherhood, even when I moved back home with my son. Our friendship continued to bridge the distance, but I was a mother now. That was something Nora had told me she never wanted for herself.

For years, we kept up contact. Sometimes there was more space between calls, but it didn't matter. Whenever we spoke, we picked up right where we left off. She visited a few times and met my kids, but it was limited. Our lives had become so different. I was a single mom of two, and she was a single woman focused on her career in the big city.

Even so, she stood by me through some of the toughest times in my life. When I had to sit in court for the trial with my husband, she was there, silently supporting me. That doesn't even touch the countless phone calls—hours spent talking, laughing, crying, confessing.

But in time, the differences became too big. The drift widened. Nora had admitted to me more than once that she envied me—my body, my appearance, my ability to do so much with so little.

The phone calls became one-sided. I only heard from her when she was in crisis. When I shared about my new entrepreneurial endeavors and things starting to take seed, it felt like she wasn't truly happy for me.

One of our last conversations still lingers in my mind. It had been a while since we talked. I said, "I don't even know where you are right now or where you're working." She replied, "Good. I want it that way—the mystery."

After that, it just drifted. No goodbye. No explanation. Just an ending.

We used to watch Grace and Frankie together, joking that it would be us one day—old, grey-haired, still hanging out, still the best of friends.

Losing her has been a quiet grief. Sometimes, I don't even realize the void it left until I feel the ache of missing her. I've thought about reaching out, but I know that's not what's needed here. I can send her love from a distance, hold our memories with tenderness, and honor that our time together evolved to an ending.

Things change. Dynamics get tired. We grow and evolve. And sometimes, people fall away too.

In the end, loving Nora taught me something I carried into every relationship that followed: that love can be expansive and wild, consuming and confusing, nourishing and wounding—all at the same time. She showed me the beauty of being seen without judgment and the ache of letting go without closure. And maybe that's what love is, at its rawest. A mirror to the parts of ourselves we are still learning to hold with tenderness. Loving her broke me open, and though it didn't last forever, the echoes of our connection still live in me, reminding me that loving deeply is never a waste. It is simply the fire that forges us into who we're becoming next.

In the wake of Nora, I carried both the ache and the awe of being fully seen. But no amount of soul recognition could prepare me for what motherhood would ask of me. Loving Nora cracked me open—but mothering my son would build something new in that open space. A fiercer kind of love. A deeper kind of surrender.

Tal

You Can't Ask a Man to Run Without Legs

I feel like I have to take a little segue here— Into the time I was alone during my pregnancy.

I was depressed. I was grieving the father I knew my son wouldn't have.

It was a strange place to be in. The in-between. Ezra and I still had contact—some back and forth. There was a lingering love. He still wanted to *show up* for me in his way, even though we were apart. But deep down, we both knew what was coming.

Around that time, I confided in a work colleague who I became quite close to. She was chatty and it was so easy to open up to her. I admired her. She was a nurse, single mom of 3 children. She was strong and capable. She told me about her friend who read tarot cards. This is when Shah came into my life. She read tarot. I went to her for a few sessions.

I'll never forget what she said.

As I poured out my story and she flipped card after card, listening deeply, she looked up and told me,

"Ezra has narcissistic traits. Although he's a brilliant man."

I didn't even know what that meant, not really. It was the first time I'd heard that word in reference to someone I'd loved. But I didn't dive into the label—because I wasn't focused on his *traits*. I was focused on the pain. On the ache of him not being able to take accountability—for me, for our child.

But what she said next burned into me and never left:

"You can't ask a man to run who doesn't have legs."

And that was it. Labels or no labels, people can only meet you to the depth they've met themselves. He couldn't take responsibility for his own life— So how could I expect him to take responsibility for the life we created?

Ultimately, I decided to move back to my hometown. Three hours away from Toronto. Closer to my mom and dad. My siblings. My support system.

So I left my life in the city— Left a comfy nursing job, Left my expressive art therapy studies, Packed it all up to go have my baby surrounded by love.

Tal's birth felt like the first time I trusted my body completely.

The contractions started late at night, creeping in like a whisper. I called my mom. She said, "Try to get some sleep — it still might be a while." But I didn't sleep. I moved.

By morning, I was cycling through every yoga pose I'd memorized from the borrowed library DVDs — prenatal yoga and breathwork that became a lifeline. I remember the rhythm of it: breathing in child's pose, grounding through cat-cow, folding over and surrendering to the waves. I wasn't afraid. I was focused. Deep inside myself, there was this quiet knowing: *You were made to do this.*

My mom stayed by my side the whole time, calm and steady. She called my older sister who came by and took one look at me and said, "You need to get to the hospital. *Now.*"

I had to stop a couple times on the way to the car. The contractions owned me — I wasn't fighting them, just breathing through, eyes closed, waiting for the peak to pass.

When we arrived, I was already 9 centimeters. No time for waiting, no time for pain meds. They wheeled me straight to the delivery room, and everything just... unfolded.

The doctor crouched between my legs, looked up with a grin and said, "This woman was made to have babies."

I laughed, even as I pushed.

And then — around 2pm, with a scream that cut through the air and into my bones — Tal was born. Wrinkled. Red. Alive. The moment he was out, I immediately broke down into tears of happiness and relief. I birthed him like a pro, like a woman remembering something ancient.

The nurses called me a birth champion. I just felt like someone who *finally trusted her body enough to let it lead.*

Tal's birth didn't just open my body — it opened my *voice.*

It's hard to explain, but something about that final push, that ancient primal scream, rewired me. It's like the sound traveled straight through my vagus nerve and shook something loose. For years, I'd felt like I couldn't quite find my voice — not just in song, but in life. But after giving birth, it felt like my throat was *freed.* My voice had depth. Confidence. Range.

I started singing more. I let myself *feel* the vibration of my own sound. I'd always loved guitar, but it used to feel like this moody, impossible companion — like I couldn't quite make peace with it.

After Tal was born, something shifted. It wasn't about perfection anymore. It was about *expression*.

That birth reconnected me — womb to throat, root to heart — and I never forgot it.

But as the joy settled and the days turned into weeks, the weight of doing it all on my own began to take shape—I was no longer just a mother, I was a single mother. It wasn't an easy road.

I was anxious. An unsure new mom, completely out of my element, crying in the dark at 3am not knowing what the hell I was doing.

And I don't know how colic works— But maybe my intuitive baby boy was already picking up on my energy. Because those first four months were *rough*.

But I learned surrender. I learned to just be still, to sit and hold my baby and soothe him. We did a lot of sitting and holding. A lot of sleeping in my arms. And somehow, we got through it.

My mom was close by, thank God. She taught me how to let go of the agendas. How to mother with presence, not perfection.

Eventually, I went back to work. I found mental health nursing jobs—commuting over an hour away just to keep a position. I'd do night shifts when I could... maybe two a week.

My health started spiraling.

Sleep-deprived. Breastfeeding. Solo-parenting. Running on fumes.

And then it happened— One snowy April morning, when you *least* expect it, I hit black ice on the highway.

I spun off and landed in the median. I wasn't physically hurt, but shaken.

I remember sitting in the car, and thinking: *"I can't do this anymore. I have a baby. I need to be here for him. This isn't sustainable."*

So I left those jobs in London—an hour and a half away. I took a break.

Around this time, I started online dating. Nothing serious—it was more like a whisper to myself: You deserve love. You deserve to see what's out there.

So I signed up for eHarmony.

And that's when *David* found me.

At first, he just poked me. A few times. I didn't respond.

He was older. He didn't even live in my country— he was from a completely different state down south.

But he kept poking. And eventually, I looked again.

Something about him felt... different. Old-fashioned. Slow in his communication. Almost sweet in a way that didn't rush or try to impress.

After weeks—maybe more—we started really talking. Emails. Stories about our lives. No pressure. Just presence.

Eventually, he suggested I come visit.

I said no. I couldn't. Not with my child and my life.

So instead, he planned a trip. All on his own.

All I saw was an image of stability. Something I hadn't felt in a long, long time.

And then, when I was raw and wide open—when I was a new mother barely keeping my head above water in sleepy little Chatham—*he* appeared.

Not with a bang or some whirlwind seduction— but with presence. With patience. With the kind of quiet steadiness and convincing energy of someone who looked like safety that I didn't know I was longing for.

I was drowning. He felt like the lifeboat.

After all the unraveling, after grief, after giving birth alone, after letting go of the life I thought I'd have...

...he didn't try to fix me, or save me, or pretend he understood the weight I was carrying.

He just met me where I was.

And slowly, gently, a new kind of love began to bloom.

Becoming a mother redefined every version of love I had ever known. It asked me to grow up quickly, to hold steady through chaos, to show up even when I was unraveling. And just when I thought I couldn't possibly carry more, love knocked again—this time wearing a different face, but still asking the same question: *Will you lose yourself again, or finally choose you?*

David: The White Night Myth

Red Flags and Red Dresses

So let's get into David—the one I married. I'll spoil it right here: the divorce lasted longer than the marriage. But let's start at the beginning.

After giving myself space to heal and move on, I dipped my toe into the world of online dating. I signed up for eHarmony. David seemed different—old-fashioned, polite, reserved... a gentleman. A Southern gentleman.

I was still young and naïve, but I shared my struggles with him. Our emails went back and forth for a couple of months. I told him how hard it was raising my son alone, how I was commuting to work, and about the car accident that really shook me. I was lucky to walk away unharmed, but it scared me enough to quit my job. I couldn't justify risking my life with a baby depending on me.

David said all the right things:
"You're not supposed to do it alone."
"Let me help you."
"Come take a break, come to my big house."

And in that moment, it sounded like paradise. I so badly wanted to escape my hometown... to escape my situation.

I left those jobs and went on unemployment for a bit. During that time, David came to visit. He scheduled a week to see me. We did it "the right way"—he booked his own accommodations.

I remember our first dinner. I wore a red dress. I felt beautiful. We met at the restaurant. I stood up, he stood up, and we hugged. It was April. He had on a wool sweater, which made me chuckle—he was overdressed. My dress was sleeveless, my legs bare.

But I kept noticing his eyes. They were so blue, and there was something gentle about him.

Later he told me, *"You were so beautiful, I couldn't take it all in."*

That week, I invited him to spend time with me and my son. It was the only way we could really get to know each other. He spent the days with us. I watched how he interacted with my son, and he watched how I mothered. He complimented me on how attentive I was—how I got down on the floor to be eye level with my little boy.

We took walks. He saw how hard it was for me—my son wanted to run, and I constantly felt on edge trying to keep him close. But it felt so good having someone with me. Someone helping.

When the week ended, saying goodbye was hard. We had some real conversations. We agreed we wanted something long-term—marriage. And even with the distance, we said we'd figure it out.

But I'll be honest: I remember sitting with David on my couch, and he said, "I sense some hesitancy in you... with affection."

He wasn't wrong. I was holding back.

David was 20 years older than me—which might sound like a lot, but coming from a relationship with a 28-year age gap, it actually felt like progress. He was attractive, stable, strong... but I wasn't feeling that spark. Maybe we just didn't have chemistry. Still, I slept with him. Partly curiosity. Partly guilt. He had come all this way, met my parents... everything had gone so smoothly.

Then I made plans to visit him.

I had interviewed for a new job—a nursing home close to home. Just minutes away. I didn't want it. I had dreaded long-term care since nursing school. The depression in those places... the way residents seemed forgotten. But the job offered 8-hour shifts and proximity.

Still, my heart wasn't in it.

So I pushed back the start date. Booked a flight to see David. But I didn't book a return flight. We were going to *play it by ear*. Deep down, I didn't want to come back. I wanted *him*.

At the border, I got flagged.

The U.S. border agents questioned me. I had my toddler with me, no return flight booked. I was nervous, unprepared. I made the mistake of handing over my phone to show my flight details. The officer scrolled through my emails.

"This is not a friend," he said.

He denied me access. I missed my flight. Lost the money.

He gave me a list of documents I'd need to prove ties to Ontario. To show I wasn't trying to move illegally.

I had to tell David. I couldn't come. I wasn't allowed.

We were both devastated. But he acted fast. Called an immigration lawyer. Got advice. The plan was: get all the documents, try again.

My mom didn't want me to go. We fought. She was right. I didn't see it then.

Looking back, it was a test. A pause. The universe trying to shake me and slow me down. But I didn't listen.

I begged for help. I was between jobs. I'd lost money. I asked my mom to help me get there—and she did. My mom and sister even crossed the border with me to make it seem more legitimate.

And so life began in Mount Pleasant, South Carolina.

David was ecstatic. He was glowing. A man in love.

But within the first few weeks, I felt it—the disconnect. He stuck to his routine, his rigid schedule, his meal prep, his quiet demeanor.

And I was alone. In a new place. Trying to navigate different roads, grocery stores that took 30 minutes to reach. Not a big deal for some, but it was so different from my little hometown.

More than that... I realized: I didn't *really* know him.

We hadn't *dated*. We had that one dinner. And now I was suddenly living in this man's house. With my son.

The stress of immigration hung over us. Pressure to get married, fast, to adjust my status.

Red flags started waving.

We had different communication styles. Emotional disconnects.

I remember being on the phone with Nora. She said, "Just come home. Take a breather. Decide from there."

So much wisdom. I didn't listen.

I felt guilty—for the legal work, the money spent, the bond my son was forming with him. He was the only father figure my child had known.

It was July. We planned to marry in August.

I *know*. Crazy. But we were told this was the fastest way to be together and start our lives.

I almost backed out. I *almost* left him.

But then...

He got down on his knees. Crying.

"It's the stress," he said. "These aren't normal circumstances. Stay the course with me. Please."

And I melted. I believed him.

So we had a quiet ceremony. Just me, him, Tal, and an officiant. My family couldn't be there—it might've raised red flags at the border.

I wore that same red dress I wore the night we met.

I tried to make the best of it. I joined mom groups. Became president when the original leader moved away. Tried to make friends. Always felt out of place.

But I loved being ten minutes from the beach and the ocean.

I spent a lot of time alone with Tal, studying for my NCLEX exam so I could work as a nurse in the States.

Underneath it all... I felt disconnected. Alone in a marriage with a man I barely knew.

And then I got pregnant. Within six months.

By then, we had returned to Ontario and finally had the wedding reception with my family and friends. That's when Jake cried with my parents—it was really over.

I was a married woman.

A housewife.

Cooking. Cleaning.

Trying to organize his house, which was filled with junk and old memories—dark closets filled with stuff from his ex-wife. Three vacuums.

I kept busy.

But I felt... utterly alone.

David didn't rescue me—but he did remind me how much I longed to be chosen. And I chased that feeling into every dynamic after, unaware that the choosing I was seeking was never theirs to give. It was always mine to claim. And so, I kept searching. Still believing that maybe next time, it would be different.

My Brief Time as a Wife

Be Seen and Not Heard

In South Carolina I made a good friend—Nadia. She and her son, Colton, became a bright spot in those quiet days. But even Nadia was only there temporarily. Her husband had a short-term contract at Boeing, and they were returning to Germany. My only real connection in Mount Pleasant wasn't even from South Carolina.

I was seven months pregnant by then. I had passed my NCLEX and was officially licensed to work in that State, but I wasn't about to dive into a job so close to giving birth—especially in a country with no paid maternity leave. Not like home, not like Canada.

So I stayed busy. Cleaning, Organizing. Painting. Nesting. Preparing. Finding problems to fix.

Trying to stay in control.

I had given up my silver Honda Civic—my first car, the one I bought on my own—when I moved to be with him. David had two vehicles: a beat-up Toyota pickup with a half-back, which I drove, and a manual Chevy Sonic he had won. The infant car seat didn't fit properly in the Toyota. I tried explaining my concerns to him. It made me miss my own car even more. I felt stupid for giving it up.

I was financially dependent, and I hated it.

One day I cried.

David transferred $700 into my account every month for groceries, but it was barely enough. I couldn't even justify buying clothes for my son or myself. Tampons felt like a luxury. I showed him the receipts through tears. He stayed quiet, scanning them. Then he said we needed to reduce grocery spending.

To be fair, I think he was overwhelmed, too. He said he was trying to absorb all the extra expenses—legal fees, life changes—without going into debt. But it didn't change how I felt: ignored. Unmet. Emotionally alone.

He had designated a time to talk about "hard things"—Sunday nights at 9 p.m.

That was it.

The rest of the week, I had to bottle it up.

I truly felt like a child again. **Be seen and not heard.**

This feels important to include, even though it's really hard for me to write about.

We were so happy when we found out I was pregnant. I remember telling him. He already had a son from his first marriage, and he admitted it would be nice to have a daughter.

But very soon into my pregnancy—just two months in—we were already having trouble communicating. I already felt like I couldn't stay. That this wasn't working. And I had this moment of panic: *I can't do this. I can't have another child if I'm leaving this man.*

I called my parents. I spoke to my mom and told her I didn't know what else to do. Of course she assured me they would help me if I kept it, but also respected and heard my choice. They were willing to come with me to get an abortion. I had actually called and scheduled it and it would have required two hour travel away from my home.

Let me tell you—this broke my heart. It was so out of alignment with my personal values. I knew the emotional damage it would cause me if I went through with it. But in that moment, it was the only relief I could find. I was truly in a state of desperation. I knew I was going to leave him eventually.

Then one day, he got a call from an adoption agency. I guess the privacy laws in South Carolina are different, because they called the house directly and spoke to him. He approached me and said, *We need to talk*. It wasn't even during our scheduled 9 p.m. Sunday conversation time. He brought me up to our bedroom while my son was napping, closed the door behind us, and told me about the call.

I was shocked. I felt like my privacy had been breached. But I told him how I felt—that I couldn't have another baby on my own. That this wasn't working. I had already asked him to do couples counselling, but he kept saying no.

And then he pleaded with me. He asked me to have the baby and leave it with him, and I could take my son and go wherever I wanted.

That moment cut me deeply. All I wanted was for him to see me. To invest in me. To care about our relationship and actually try to make it work. But in that moment, I felt like a vessel. Like a body. Like a surrogate.

All I could say to him was, *You don't know what kind of mother I am*. I walked out of the room.

After that conversation, I knew deep down I wouldn't be able to go through with the abortion. And in my typical way of smoothing things over, I went back down to him and said, *I'm not going to go* through with it. But I pleaded with him again: *We need to work on this. We need to fix this.*

Of course, nothing changed.

Then one day, everything unraveled.

It was mid-summer, humid and stifling. I was swollen, uncomfortable, big with pregnancy, and invisible in my own home. I hadn't felt David *see* me in months. He barely looked at me. We existed like polite roommates. And I was tired of pretending.

That day, I stayed home and took photos of the infant car seat, showing how it didn't fit in the Toyota. I was in tears. I sent them to him while he was at work. He never responded.

That weekend, before our "scheduled" talk time, I brought it up anyway.

"Can we talk about the vehicles?" I asked. My voice shook a little. I was genuinely scared. Two kids, one of them a newborn, no safe way to drive us around.

David shrugged. "You can drive the Sonic."

I blinked. "It's a manual. I don't know how to drive manual."

"Well," he said, "you can learn."

"I'm *eight months* pregnant. That's a lot of pressure right now."

He didn't budge. "We're not buying another car. We have two. We'll make it work."

Something inside me snapped. Quietly. Powerfully.

"This isn't a marriage," I said. "This is a dictatorship."

And just like that, I knew.

I was done.

I told him I needed space. Separation.

I called my mom.

The very next day, I was on a plane—my son beside me, my daughter still in the womb.

David drove us to the airport.

When I asked, he agreed.

He didn't put up much of a fight.

There was no dramatic goodbye. No last plea. Just a quiet letting go.

It wasn't the ending I imagined—but maybe it was the one I needed. I had spent so long hoping he would fight for me, for us. But in the end, I had to be the one to fight for myself.

And so I came home—not just to a place, but to a reckoning. A reckoning with who I had become, who I was becoming, and what it would take to rebuild a life from the fragments.

Rory Grace

♥

Coming Home, Starting Over

I remember getting home and just feeling *broken*.

Here I was—again. Back in the exact place I had tried so hard to avoid.

I thought I was doing the right thing. I really believed I was fixing something for my son—trying to give him a father. That was the root of it, wasn't it? Guilt. Fear of not being enough for him. This aching need to protect him from the kind of fatherless childhood I had dreaded for him.

But here we were. Again.

And this time—it was worse.

I wasn't just a single mom to one child now. I had another on the way. I had left my husband, and he was fourteen hours away. I remember sitting in my mom's living room—surrounded by her, my younger siblings, and my brother's boyfriend at the time—and just sobbing.

How did this happen again?
How was I going to survive this?

The drama didn't vanish overnight. It never does.
I had nothing when I got back from the U.S.

When your residency status changes like that, you lose all your provincial coverage in Ontario. No health card. No public access to free obstetrics care. I had to pay out of pocket for every appointment, then fight for reimbursement from an American insurance company. It was a mess.

I was riddled with anxiety—not the kind most moms have before a second baby—but the kind that settles deep in your chest and whispers, *you're alone again.*

I grieved the transition.
I grieved not just the end of my marriage—but the loss of life as it was with my little boy, Tal. Our one-on-one bond was about to shift, and I didn't know how to hold that.

No car. No job.
I even had to start the process to reinstate my nursing license to be active again.

But I went one day at a time.
I was under my parents' roof. I had support. And slowly, I started the process of rebuilding.

I reinstated my nursing license.
I went to every OB appointment.
I made plans for when it was time to give birth—Tal would stay with my sister at my parents' place.

And then the day came.

It started as a slow leak. I remember being at the park with Tal, making sure he didn't chase the Canadian geese, when I felt the trickle each time I squatted down to pick him up.

I knew.

But I was scared. Being a nurse makes you the worst kind of patient.

That night, I tucked Tal into bed, and at midnight, I finally gave in and went to the hospital. The nurses rolled their eyes when I said I thought my water was leaking. I told them my son came fast—they didn't believe me.

They checked me.

"Only three centimeters," they said.

But within an hour, everything changed.

I advanced fast. I think it surprised them.

They rushed me down to labor and delivery.

Then the fever hit.

It was nothing like my labor with Tal. I was terrified. My body burned, and I felt out of control. David showed up. He was trying to be supportive in his own way, but I didn't feel emotionally connected to him anymore, if I ever did. I barely noticed him except when he kept squeezing the hand with my IV, and it hurt.

But there was this nurse—this angel—who took my other hand and did this lovely massage.

At one point, I truly thought I was going to die. I couldn't have the usual pain meds because of my fentanyl allergy. I was in so much pain, I cried out:

"I can't do this. I need something."

She squeezed my hand, looked me in the eyes, and said,

"You *can* do this. You *have* to do this."

And I did.

Somewhere around 2:30 a.m., Rory Grace was born.

And I didn't die.

I asked my mom, "is she okay?"

I hadn't heard her cry. She was quiet.

But then my baby girl was laid on my chest and I fell in love for a second time.

Those first few months are a blur.

I was grateful. Deeply grateful.

For my mom. For my dad. For being under the same roof as people who loved me.

Slowly, I adjusted to life as a mother of two—juggling a newborn and a three-year-old.

Then, when Rory was about four months old, I felt it:

The pull toward my independence.

I wanted to parent my children without all the noise—without everyone else's voices, however well-intentioned.

I started looking. For work. For housing.
I found a job in visiting nursing.

I needed a car—my dad helped me find the right one.
I found a charming two-bedroom apartment in the upper floor of a house. It was simple. No washer or dryer. Mattresses on the floor. But it was cozy. It was ours. It was **home.**

We moved in when Rory was about four months old and Tal was three.

Those early days back home weren't easy. I was healing while mothering, grieving while growing. But there was a tenderness to it all—a kind of sacred slowness that allowed me to soften.

The apartment wasn't much, but it held us. It held our laughter, our chaos, our beginnings. I was learning how to be a mother of two, how to stand on my own again, how to feel safe in my body and life.

And just as I began to feel that safety return, something else arrived. Or rather—*someone*.

That's when I met Sam.

Sam's Story

♥

When Stability Shows Up

I met Sam one spring day when I was outside with the kids, and a familiar, tall, good-looking man approached me. The truth is, I recognized him right away. When I was in high school, he worked there—I was just 16 then, and I later learned he would've been 35.

Even back then, his presence stood out. I remember one moment in particular: I was sitting in English class with one of the strictest and most feared teachers at the school—short, sharp-witted, Lebanese, and known for enforcing the uniform policy with zero tolerance. People said she was just mean, but I always thought it was a bit of a façade. She was brilliant and fiercely opinionated. Anyway, I digress. One day, Sam walked into that classroom, and I noticed right away that even *she* flirted with him. That presence of his—it was magnetic. I remember thinking he was so good-looking for an older man.

And now, here he was, nearly 15 years later. I was 32, and he was 51.

It started innocently. Sam asked if we could share the internet—since we lived in the same old house, he figured there was no need for a separate installation. He offered to pay me monthly and use our Wi-Fi. Being tight on cash, I agreed.

We didn't become friends right away. He was friendly, sure, but in truth, he befriended my kids before me. He had that natural ease with children—his deep, distinct voice, the way he carried himself. My son, especially, really liked him.

He asked a few times if I wanted to come down to the porch for a drink or just to chat. I always politely declined. I knew in my gut it wasn't a good idea. We were neighbors, and I didn't want to blur those lines.

A side note—Jake had come to visit me around that time. He met both my children. Even if our contact was sporadic, we always found our way back to each other somehow. I remember telling him, "My neighbor downstairs... I think he's into me." Jake just looked at me and said, **"Heather, don't fuck your neighbor."**

Around that same time, Jake and I shared a tender moment—not in a sexual way, but in a deeply emotional one. We sat in the car and kissed, shared how we still loved each other so much and always would. After the kiss, he said, **"There's just nothing like it."** That moment stuck with me.

Meanwhile, I had started therapy and had finally decided to file for divorce. I took my time with that decision. My husband had come to visit us, but it felt off. I wasn't willing to go back. It felt too late. He even called my therapist, without my permission, to finally inquire about couples' sessions.

Let's be clear—I had asked him to go to couples counseling at least three times before I left him in South Carolina. His efforts came too little, too late. Even months later, he said, "I just think you're amazing. Come back. I'll have that SUV in the driveway." But the door had already closed.

Back to Sam. I was officially separated. Divorce papers had been served. David had gone silent—no contact for six months. I started dating again. I met someone online and went out a few times. It didn't work out, but we became friends—and still are, nine years later. He was going through a divorce, too, and we connected over our shared experiences.

Meanwhile, Sam kept showing up—brushing snow off my car, inviting me down for a chat, doing neighborly things that started to feel like more. Still, I kept my distance. Until one especially rough week at work when I made my first noticeable medication error. The patient was okay, but the weight of the mistake crushed me. I spiraled. The responsibility of being a nurse, the power I held—it hit me hard.

That was the moment I finally said yes to Sam's invitation. That night, everything between us shifted. From the very beginning, our emotional connection was easy. We talked for hours. He was a flirt, but more than that—he admired me. He told me how he watched me carry a baby on one hip, holding my son's hand with the other, loading them into the car like a supermom, and admiring how pretty I was while doing it.

He respected me. And I resisted.

Eventually, a better rental came along—standalone home, huge yard, separate rooms for the kids, near the school I wanted. It was the perfect place. Once there were definite plans to move, I thought: maybe now it's safe. I let my guard down. Things progressed quickly with Sam.

He was coming out of a divorce too. He'd gone through something unimaginably painful—his eldest daughter had died from cancer. We talked about grief and life and divorce. He sat beside me through court dates and emotional breakdowns. He helped move us into the new place, and again, things moved fast.

He always wanted more than I could give. If I'd let him, he would've moved in. But I wasn't ready. Deep down, I felt like he was trying to fill a void—his family breaking, his daughter gone. And I knew my family couldn't be the solution to that pain.

By then, I'd started to recognize my own core wound: the belief that I wasn't enough on my own—not for my son, not for my daughter, not for myself. I was determined to prove that wrong.

So whenever Sam inched closer, I'd pull back. I set boundaries. I told him he couldn't just show up unannounced. And yet—his love language was acts of service. He built our play structure. Mowed the lawn. Fixed things around the house. It was easy to love someone like that. He was the epitome of a family man.

He became a strong father figure to my children—even before he and I were romantically involved. And once we were, things deepened. We did everything with the kids. It felt like we were a family. But despite all of that, I kept him at arm's length. There was always that push-pull tension.

We were on and off from 2017 until 2021. Sam became my best friend—and yet, deep down, I couldn't picture a future where he moved in, where we built a life together. Something was missing.

Over time, things got complacent. He'd come over after the kids were asleep. That was our relationship—limited, private. I grew bored. I told him we never did anything anymore. I tried to reignite the spark, but I noticed his grief came in cycles. Around his daughter's birthday, the anniversary of her passing, or Christmas—he'd retreat.

And though I understood, it hurt. My kids depended on him by then. It felt like he was taking that for granted.

So one day, I just ended it. Over the phone. I said, "This isn't working anymore." It was the cleanest cut I'd ever made.

A month later, he went to Cuba with another woman—someone who had also lost a child. They bonded over that. It made sense. But it still hurt. I thought about all the trips Sam had wished we could take as a family—things that never happened because of my financial limitations, my job, the reality of single motherhood.

I know I said earlier the break up was a clean cut, but Sam and I forged a friendship about 2 years post breakup. Sam — always lingering at the edges of my life like an unfinished chapter. He has been an emotional connection I could slip into so easily – familiar, safe, soft. Even after all the time apart, he remained a presence, a safety net I could lean into when everything else felt unstable. There was comfort in knowing he was there, someone who saw me in my darkest days and still chose to love me through them. But as I've grown, I've started to question whether this lingering connection is love or simply the comfort of what is known. I see now that holding onto him, even as a friend, has been a way of keeping myself tethered to an old version of who I was – a woman who needed someone to catch her if she fell. And maybe, just maybe, breaking that connection is how I finally learn to catch myself.

Letting go of Sam wasn't just about him. It was about releasing the version of me that still believed I needed saving.

It was the first time I began to trust that I could hold *me*. That I didn't have to reach for a hand every time the ground shook beneath me.

And in that space—raw, uncertain, quiet—I began to hear something else. Not a voice, but a sensation. A whisper from within. A knowing that had been there all along.

It was time to come home to my body.

What My Body Always Knew

The Lesson of Eddie

I've been stalling on this chapter—maybe because it's still unraveling inside of me. Maybe because Eddie wasn't just another love. He was the mirror. He *was* the wound. The catalyst that cracked me open to the deepest root I still hadn't healed.

This one... this one is hard to write.
But I need to.

I need to tell the truth, especially to myself—so that when the part of me starts romanticizing the past, I can remember what really happened. So I don't go back to illusions. So I don't forget.

I loved him.
Freely. Recklessly.
I gave too much—trying to be chosen, seen, held, kept.

But that kind of love—mine—was born from lack.
I was still trying to earn what I never believed I was worthy of.
So I tolerated behavior I should've walked away from. Disrespect.

Emotional immaturity. Gaslighting.

Because I was afraid. Afraid to be alone. Afraid to start over. Afraid that no one would ever truly love me.

And yet—I knew.

From the beginning, I knew.

The red flags were there.

There was a heaviness around him. Unprocessed trauma. A restlessness in his spirit.

A carelessness in his words.

An inability to sit still with discomfort, or be fully present.

There was surface charm—but he could not access the deeper soul-sharing I craved.

And my soul... my body... they need depth. They long to be met in the in-between.

But I ignored that, because his arms felt good. His weight on top of me felt grounding.

His lips fit mine.

The sexual chemistry was real.

But so was the pain.

He lied to me—especially about sex.

He withheld information, played things down, omitted truths.

And his deception robbed me of informed consent. That's a kind of betrayal people don't talk about enough.

I overshared from the beginning.

Assumed vulnerability would be met with vulnerability.

Assumed honesty would be matched with honesty.

I showed him my work—my sensual embodiment, my movement, my sacred play—not from arrogance, but from a place of needing him to understand: *This is who I am.*

It was like I was silently pleading: *Please don't leave me. See me and stay. Accept and approve of what I do. Love me please.*

And in doing that… I abandoned myself.

He mirrored the shame I hadn't yet healed.

And I tried to prove my worth.

Tried to be enough.

Tried to earn love by being endlessly available.

He gaslit me.

Dismissed my emotions.

Walked away, again and again.

He love-bombed.

Then went silent.

Objectified me.

Consumed me.

Even in all of its chaos, there were moments of tenderness—real connection and emotional bonding. We shared a deep mutual understanding of what it's like to raise a child alone, without the other parent's involvement.

Maybe that's why I kept making excuses for his behaviour. For him not stepping up, for not showing up fully for me, for not embracing the wholeness of who I am and the life I carry.

It started fun and light, and we gave in to the sexual chemistry.

But even in the bedroom, something was missing.

And here, I digress.

The Mirror in the Bedroom

There's something I'm finally learning to name without shame: the ways I've been *underloved* in the bedroom.

Not just physically.
Emotionally.
Energetically.
Spiritually.

That's the deeper wound. And Eddie became the mirror for all of it.

He reached out again after another stretch of silence. And of course, it was sexual. Again.
That's when it finally clicked—he wasn't reaching for *me*.
Not the woman who cracked open in front of him.
Not the one who stayed. Who listened. Who gave.
He reached for what was easy.
For the part of me he could *consume* without having to connect.

And the hardest part?
Sex was already where some of my greatest pain lived.
I needed more.
More presence. More devotion. More reverence.
But every time I voiced that, he shut down.
Made it about him.
Felt attacked.
Suddenly *my need* became *his shame*, and I was left holding both.

We were limited in our sex life.
I couldn't explore the full expression of my sexuality.
I started to feel disconnected from it.
I started to feel like I didn't want it at all.
And that terrified me.

It started early in our relationship, he would film our intimate sessions. I suppose it was fun and exciting at first. Then it stopped being fun for me. I was craving presence and connection. And he habitually recorded us.

I started speaking up and finding my voice again. He didn't like when I set boundaries.

He wanted his quick fix before leaving—like I was a to-do list item, not a woman.

He wasn't present.

He was entitled.

And I kept trying.

Trying to recreate the chemistry.

Trying to feel something that was already slipping through my hands.

But I was shutting down.

And this hit me like a wave:

I've had to ask *every* man I've been with to go down on me.

My ex-husband.

Sam.

Eddie.

And while I've gotten braver in asking, faster at naming what I want—

the fact that I've had to *ask* at all…

That's the wound.

Because it's not about the act.

It's about the energy.

The care.

The intention.

I shouldn't have to ask.

I shouldn't have to wonder if my pleasure is *worth it*.

I shouldn't have to convince someone that my body deserves to be adored.

That's the mirror Eddie held up.

He taught me—painfully and completely—that if a man can't meet me in the bedroom,
he can't hold me anywhere else.

Not emotionally.
Not spiritually.
Not truly.

And this isn't just about sex.
It's about how we, as women, have been conditioned to shrink.
To silence our bodies.
To apologize for having needs.
To feel like asking for more is *too much*.

But I'm not carrying that anymore.
My body is not too much.
My needs are not too much.
My pleasure is not negotiable.

And next time?
I won't ask.
I'll already know.

I haven't told the full story about Eddie. Maybe because it still sits in my chest like a stone I can't swallow. Or maybe because I've been too afraid and ashamed to admit it out loud. I shared with a couple close friends. But I feel like my story is so relatable and vulnerability prevails again.

But the truth is, it wasn't just the gaslighting or the emotional abuse. It was the porn.

He lied to me about it. From the beginning.

I remember asking him directly, lying on my bed together, my heart pounding in that sickening way it does when you're about to betray yourself by staying quiet. I hadn't planned to ask, but I was already noticing something. From the very beginning, there was difficulty—he struggled to get hard for penetration. I noticed he was rushing things, going straight for that without any buildup or foreplay. I tried to create arousal, to fix it, to make it okay. He told me it had happened in his last relationship too. A pattern, he said. I tried to be compassionate, to hold space, but quietly, my own emotions were stirring. I hadn't experienced this with a partner before. A question I didn't want to ask formed in my gut: *Is he just not attracted to me in real life?*

That's why I inquired about porn. I needed to understand. I needed something to make it make sense.

He said he didn't use porn anymore. That he didn't need it when he was in a relationship. That he didn't even want it.

That was his word: "I don't use it when I'm in a relationship." Instead, he said he just needed to get used to me.

And I believed him.

So when he started recording me—us—I thought it was different. Special. I thought it was because he wanted *me*. Because he enjoyed *me*. Because it turned him on knowing he could watch *me* when we were apart.

But it wasn't that.

It was porn.

He turned *me* into porn. And the whole time, he was still watching other imagery, other porn. Consuming it. Using it to get off while telling me he didn't.

I feel so sick when I think about it now. Because I let him record me. Over and over. I never spoke up. I thought I was being the "cool girl," the one who didn't care, the one who was sexually free and open and easy to love because I didn't have boundaries.

And it wasn't that I didn't want to say no. It was that I thought if I did, he'd leave. He'd find someone else. Someone who would give him what I wouldn't.

I feel disgusted when I think about it now. The biggest betrayal wasn't just that he lied to me about porn. It was that he made *me* complicit in it. That he robbed me of informed consent. That I believed his lie so deeply I let him record me under false pretenses.

That's what makes it feel so *icky*, so humiliating, so violating.

I know I'm not the only woman who's felt this or experienced this. Who's been told, "It's just for me," only to find out it never was. Who's believed, "I need this because I can't have you right now," only to find out you were just another folder in a device full of strangers.

I'm afraid to share this because it feels shameful. Because I'm worried people will judge me for letting him record me at all. But I know there are women who need to hear it. Women who need to know it's not their shame to carry. That lies strip away the power of consent. That this is a violation, even if it wasn't forced. Because it was forced through deception.

And I'm done being silent about it.

Silence protected him. But speaking is what sets *me* free.

Naming it—what happened, what it meant, what it cost—became a portal. Not just to healing, but to remembering. Remembering that my body always knew. That my worth was never up for negotiation. That love should never come with a hidden price.

But some lessons come wrapped in illusion.

And the next one… would come dressed as devotion, disguised as depth, echoing every wound I had yet to name.

That was Eddie.

Eddie and the Echoes

Unraveling the Urge to Check

I discovered his lie one day. He didn't confess on his own—I caught him. I saw it on his phone, a porn video he claimed a friend had sent. But from there, everything unraveled.

I felt the sharp sting of betrayal, my trust breaking into pieces I couldn't hold together. In his typical fashion, he got up to leave. And even in that moment, as I stood there gutted, I still tried to soothe him. I still tried to fix it.

It's ridiculous when I think about it now. I should have let him walk out that day and never seen him again. But I didn't. I gave it another month or two, telling myself we could work through it. We got on the waitlist for couples counselling. But even then, he told me, "I don't think we need to talk about that there. I'm not comfortable with a stranger knowing this."

He said he was going to stop using it. Blamed his marriage. Said his ex-wife had shamed him, and that's why he lied—consistently. But he kept focusing on the porn, as if that were the core issue. I didn't believe him. I said, *"Can you stop making promises you can't keep? Can we just let this be out in the open now?"*

What hurt most wasn't the porn. It was the lying. The deception from the very beginning. And no matter how many times we talked about it, I felt like he just wasn't grasping that part.

Deep down, I knew. I knew therapy wouldn't help if he was already micromanaging what I could say. If he wasn't willing to show up fully, there was nothing to save.

One day, he came over. My body was already screaming at me that I couldn't keep going like this—performing, giving, ignoring my own truth. I tried to open up a conversation with him about a book I was reading on female pleasure. What I really wanted was to bring his attention back to *me*—to presence over performance.

But he got defensive. He said I sounded like a teacher trying to educate him. He insisted he knew about women's anatomy.

In that moment, all I could think was—I don't care about other women's anatomy. Or about all these women he watched in porn videos. I want my partner to care about *me*. My body. What turns *me* on. My nervous system. My emotions. In my experience, if I don't feel emotionally safe with a man, I won't cum. It's that simple.

I finally told him, "You know what? I don't feel like having sex with you right now. Or in an hour. Or in a few hours. So what do you want to do today?"

Because let's be honest. That's what he always came for. I can't even remember a time when we didn't.

When I said I wasn't going to sleep with him, he started to walk out again. And something inside me snapped. I screamed from downstairs, "Yeah, leave. Show me your back again. You do that so well. Keep showing me who you are."

He must have changed his mind because he came back. But he looked lost. He kept following me around the house, blocking my path while I carried a laundry basket. I just wanted him out of my face and my space. I was so angry.

I told him to move. To get out of my way. To get out of my house.

But he wasn't listening. He kept trying to come closer, like he wanted to hug me. But I didn't want a hug. I wanted to be heard. Seen. Felt. Understood.

So I screamed. I screamed from a place so deep it cracked open something ancient inside me.

"Get the fuck out of my house."

And that was it. That was how it ended. That was how the silence began.

Except, it wasn't really the end.

Even after that final blowout, even after two months of silence, I still felt the pull. The energetic tether between us was so strong it wrapped itself around my body, coiling in my gut like a snake. I couldn't stop checking him on social media. Even when I wasn't speaking to him, I was still looking, still searching for signs that I mattered, that he was hurting too, that I still held a place in his world.

He kept reaching out through burner accounts, and I stayed strong and silent—until I didn't. After two months of keeping him blocked and ignoring every attempt, I reopened the door. I invited him back in, telling myself we needed to have a "real conversation" without drama and screaming.

I don't even know why. Maybe I wanted a calmer ending, something amicable and mutual. Maybe I needed to see it clearly, to prove to myself that nothing had changed. Maybe I still hoped he would choose me in the way I longed for. Or maybe I was still clinging to the scraps of a fantasy, the hope that love meant staying, enduring, forgiving.

But deep down, I already knew.

When he came back, it felt good for a moment. Like relief. Like the ache softened. But quickly, the same old patterns resurfaced. The same emptiness. The same sense that I was just a body to him, never a heart.

I remember lying beside him, feeling lonelier than I ever did alone.

That's when it finally clicked.

I wasn't reopening it to heal us.

I was reopening it to finally close it for myself.

Because love isn't supposed to feel like that.

And I wasn't willing to abandon myself again.

Craving Proof

♥

In the silence, he still mattered—and in a digital world where presence is measured in pings and posts, that absence was deafening. And that's where I have had to dive deeper.

So here I go.

In the silence, in the void... I checked to see that he was still there. A sliver of reassurance. A familiar feeling. His face. His torso. His muscles. Even the cryptic, subtle emotional bait he had been leaving for weeks.

I wanted to feel seen. I wanted to feel missed.

So every time I read a post that felt like it was meant for me—it affirmed he still loved me, even in his distorted, limited way.

I was afraid if I stopped checking, that's the last thread. The final line of indirect communication.

Was it abandonment I feared? Probably. That's the deeper wound.

When the urge to check hit me, my brain was clawing for closure, trying to make sense of it all. Was he hurting? Had he moved on? Did he realize the pain he caused me? Was he taking accountability yet?

My body felt the anxiety first— a buzzing in my gut, a restlessness. A compulsion.

And yet, when I did check... it felt *familiar*.

I checked when we were together too.

It was a source of so much pain—so much comparison. Especially on TikTok. The women he followed, the accounts he engaged with. And the truth is, I hadn't even thought to look. But his constant accusations—about me, my integrity, my work—started to wear me down. He accused me of being inappropriate with my subscribers, of being too sensual, too exposed. He said he supported my work—but he didn't. Not really.

He liked the *idea* of it. The fantasy. But the reality of my sensuality—how I embodied it— made him uncomfortable.

He used to say we were perfectly matched. Physically. Sexually. And in many ways, we were.

There was a deep, natural chemistry from the beginning. I remember our first hug. Being in his arms. Feeling like I had arrived, feeling like I was home.

He was the shortest man I'd ever dated—just an inch or two taller than me. But it didn't matter. His bulk, his width, the solidity of him… it made me feel safe.

It was novel to me. I'd never been with a man built like that. Strength and definition.

So when he brought up his jealousy—about a year ago this time—it exploded. I called out the double standard. How could he shame me for my work when he was admiring and following other attractive women, consuming them in the same way he imagined my subscribers consumed me?

That was our first big break. I ended it. Six weeks apart.

He still messaged. I didn't block him that time. Breadcrumbs. Just enough to keep me tethered.

But he never really took responsibility. He got defensive. Dismissed my feelings. And I accepted the crumbs, maybe because I was afraid— afraid I wouldn't find anyone else who could *accept* what I do.

Maybe that fear came from Eddie— how he chipped away at me, made me feel shame about my sensuality.

I started to doubt myself. Had I *overreacted*? Was I being *insecure*? Wasn't it *normal* for people to be attracted to others? Did that really mean he was disloyal if he was just looking, and not acting?

So I went back.

But that last time—after the final blowout, when I screamed, reclaimed my voice, told him to get the fuck out— I blocked him.

I blocked him everywhere I could. And I kept him blocked.

But I checked a few days later. Of course I did.

And there it was—he was following a new TikTok account. A woman who represented the kind of beauty I don't embody— breast implants, lip filler, model thin. I compared myself immediately. I saw only flaws, inadequacies.

It *broke* me. It made me feel sick.

Before that when we were still together, I noticed he'd unfollowed those types of accounts. He cleaned up his feed—said he cared, that he heard me.

So to see that... just days after the breakup? It felt like a gut punch. Like it was *intentional*. Like he wanted to get a reaction. Or this is just him showing who he truly is.

Four days into silence, I wondered— *Is this bait?* Is he trying to see if I still care?

But I didn't respond. Not that time.

I couldn't block him on X (formerly Twitter) though and this became a kind of silent battlefield.

I was processing pain publicly on my feed, secretly hoping he'd read it and *finally* see me. Understand the harm. Validate my heartbreak.

If he left a comment or tweeted something—anything— it would mean that it was real. That two years meant *something*.

Maybe this all echoes the wound Jake left.

That first love. That primal heartbreak. Not being chosen.

But then, years later—hearing Jake's mom tell my mom: "*Jake will always love Heather.*"

Or Jake himself, years after the fact— admitting he never stopped loving me. That he always will.

Or hearing from my parents that he cried—*cried*—at my wedding.

It gave me this distorted validation. That I was lovable... even when I wasn't chosen.

Maybe it goes even further back than Jake. But I can't access childhood right now.

What I *could* feel is that little girl inside.

The one who needed to check—because she's not okay if she didn't. She whispers things like:

"*If I don't check, how will I know I still mattered?*"
"*If he disappears completely, maybe I really didn't mean anything.*"
"*If I see him sad or missing me, maybe I can finally feel validated.*"
"*If I know what he's doing, I can protect myself.*"

But these urges—they were not just about him.

They were about my nervous system screaming for resolution. Because trauma bonds don't end with clarity. They end with chaos. Withdrawal. Craving. Confusion.

The Truth

After the big blowout and the two month silence, I revisited us for a couple weeks. Maybe I needed to feel it again, to test if anything had changed, to see if he could finally meet me where I've always been waiting. But the truth kept echoing back to me:

He cannot meet me.

The patterns were still there. The boundary pushing. The defensiveness. The lack of attunement to my heart's truth. My body felt it before my mind could even form the words. That sinking feeling in my belly. The ache in my chest. The heavy contraction each time he minimized my pain or tried to brush away my tears with his discomfort.

I told him calmly this time: *I care for and love you deeply. But I think it's best for me to step away now. I can't keep reopening wounds my soul is asking me to finally close.*

And he said "*okay babe, be well.*" Later he messaged, *nothing left but to cry here I suppose.* And I didn't respond.

Because I realized… I always respond. I always reach back to soothe him in his discomfort, even when he is the one who caused mine. This time, I let the silence hold me instead.

The next day, the rage was still there—still burning, still craving resolution. So I sent him one final message. I asked him to delete the personal content he still had—videos and photos I had created for my work, pieces of myself I had once shared with him in trust. I told him I wasn't comfortable with him keeping them anymore. I needed to reclaim what I could. To draw a final boundary. To stand for myself, one last time.

His response was everything I needed to see. He turned cruel. He threw words meant to degrade me, to reduce me to nothing but a body for his consumption. In the end, his mask slipped completely. There was no tenderness, no remorse, no understanding of the harm he had caused. Only bitterness, insults, and a final attempt to devalue me as I walked away.

And with that, I knew: This *was* closure. Silence would be my final word. He was a soul lesson. It was time to let him go.

He told me once, *I cannot look at you if you're not mine.*

But I was never his. I belong to myself. I always have. And that's the part that scared him the most.

This is what I know now:

I glow up when I am no longer navigating someone's frequent mishaps. When I no longer have to shrink my knowing to keep the peace. When I no longer tolerate what my soul cannot.

The first time I ended it, I stayed tethered. I checked his profiles. I looked for signs. I held onto hope that he would come back changed.

This time, the no contact is real. Because this time, *I am not leaving to get him back*. I am leaving to get **me** back.

Maybe that's the ending I always needed:

Not the dramatic screaming. Not the forced goodbye. But the quiet closing of a door that no longer leads me home.

And so I choose myself again. Over and over. Every day. Until the echoes fade and my own voice is all that remains.

The echoes take their time. They linger. But eventually, even they grow quiet

Even after we walk away, there's a part of us still listening—for the ding of a message, the shift in a gaze, the apology that never comes. We crave proof that the love was real, that we mattered, that the pain meant something.

But what if the proof was never theirs to give?

What if the proof is in the leaving? In the not-checking. In the boundary we hold. In the way we choose ourselves—again and again—until the ache softens and self-trust rises to meet us.

That's what I've learned.

And if you're here, still tangled in the longing or the loss, I want to offer you what I wish someone had offered me...

What follows is my raw dive into why I checked, what it gave me, and what part of me it protected. It is here, in this void of silence, that the impulse to reach for my phone became the last thread of connection I clung to. If you see yourself in me, maybe this can help you process what is underneath the compulsion.

1. The Familiar Pull

In the stillness, I reach—not out loud, but through screens and silent scrolls—searching for signs that he's still there. A flicker of his face, the curve of his arm, a cryptic post that feels like it could be for me. It's not just about him; it's about familiarity. The comfort of recognition. The hope of being seen, of being missed. And when I stumble across something that feels like a breadcrumb, I grip it tightly—telling myself he still loves me, in the only way he knows how.

Insight: *This pull to check is not weakness; it's your nervous system craving resolution from an unresolved bond.*

2. What Checking Gives Me—and Takes Away

Connection vs. Chaos: Checking makes me feel connected, but it also reopens old wounds of comparison and insecurity. On TikTok, I saw new accounts he followed—women who didn't look like me. I felt the sting of inadequacy.

Validation vs. Doubt: Each subtle notification offers a hit of validation: a comment, a like, a fleeting sign that I still matter. But then the doubt floods back: *Is this enough? Is it real?*

Control vs. Chaos: Urges arise in the gut, with anxiety and restlessness. Checking feels familiar because it was part of our relationship ritual. It was how I learned if he cared.

Reflection: *I'm not just checking on him; I'm checking on my own worth.*

3. Echoes of the Past

It brings me back to Jake—my first love—and that early wound of not being chosen. His mother once told mine, *"Jake will always love Heather,"* and years later, Jake admitted he never truly stopped loving me. At the time, those words felt like proof. They fed a deep craving I didn't yet understand: the belief that if someone still wanted me after everything, then I was worthy. That love, even delayed or withheld, could somehow validate my value.

Connection: *The part of me that checks now is that same little girl who needed proof that she mattered.*

4. The Internal Conversation

When the urge to check rises, it's not just about him—it's a voice within me seeking certainty, safety, significance. It whispers doubts and what-ifs, disguised as protection:

- *"I just need to know where I stand."*

- *"Maybe there's still something unspoken between us."*

- *"If he's hurting too, then it wasn't all in my head."*

- *"If I stay aware, I won't be blindsided again."*

These thoughts aren't logical—they're survival strategies. The mind trying to soothe the ache the heart hasn't yet fully released. But understanding them now allows me to meet them with compassion, not compulsion.

I understand these fears now as echoes of attachment wounds. But they no longer serve me.

5. Honoring and Redirecting the Urge

I no longer shame this part of me—the one who wanted to know, to feel seen, to feel chosen. I honor her. I sit beside her in the silence and say:

"Thank you for trying to protect me. I know you were scanning the horizon for danger, searching for signs of love, for any proof that we still mattered. But we don't need to chase that anymore. I am here now. I see you. I choose you. You are worthy, even in the quiet. You matter, even when unseen."

This is not about denial—it's about devotion. A sacred redirection.

It's not punishment to stop checking. It's reverence. It's choosing my wholeness over the hollow echo of uncertainty.

This is an internal vow I make again and again:

"I choose peace over panic. Truth over fantasy. Wholeness over craving. I don't stop checking because I don't care— I stop because I finally do."

6. Moving Forward

The urge to check is both a wound and a compass—it shows me where healing still lives. It shows me where I need more compassion, curiosity, and self-trust. As I write these words, I am already healing.

Invitation to the Reader:
- Notice where you check in your own life.
- Ask yourself: What am I hoping to gain or protect?
- Offer that part of you love and a new choice: *"I am enough, and I choose me."*

This chapter is for every woman who has found herself reaching for a phone in the quiet, hoping a notification would prove her worth. May you find in these pages the courage to unfollow the old loop and the grace to reclaim your own energy.

At some point, the craving quiets.

Not because the longing vanishes, but because we finally remember: we are the proof. Our presence. Our peace. Our glow.

And from that remembering, something begins to rise—an inner standard, shaped not by how others treat us, but by how deeply we've come to value ourselves.

Speaking that standard isn't easy. It requires clarity. It requires courage. And it requires the willingness to lose people who were never truly aligned.

But it's worth it. Because our boundaries are not walls—they are invitations for real love to meet us where we now stand.

Speaking the Standard

There are moments when the body speaks before the mind catches up. Moments when clarity rises—not through logic—but through exhaustion, ache, and undeniable knowing.

This was one of those moments.

I have felt the energy of the masculine around me—not just from the past, but from the present. From the men I've released and the ones who've recently appeared. Some have lingered as ghosts. Some have circled back. Some have offered glimmers but no ground. And I need to speak this out loud.

Eddie. We know his name. He still holds the strongest energetic tether, even after everything. The pull of him was deep, complex, karmic. He was 15 years older than me. Like my ex-husband, who was 20 years older. That pattern is not accidental. I see now how I once equated age with safety, with being taken care of—only to find that emotional maturity doesn't always follow physical years.

Eddie reached in and stirred something raw in me. And he also revealed every part of a man I cannot hold space for anymore. The inconsistency. The sexualization. The avoidance of emotional depth. The inability to truly listen, especially when I spoke my needs around intimacy. Our sex life became where I shut down. He didn't meet me there, and worse—he acted entitled to access I didn't feel safe giving. That truth, as painful as it is, remains one of the most important mirrors he gave me.

Then there's **Ryan**. A man from my past, who remembers me from high school. He calls me the first woman who gave him sass, but with admiration. He reappeared recently with warm energy, openness, and a gentle tone that made me feel like I could tell him anything. And that mattered. But there's something missing. He talks a lot. He has ideas, suggestions, excitement. But little follow-through. And I've learned that words without action are not safe. He doesn't harm me, but he doesn't hold me either. And I deserve to be held.

Then there's **Tyler**. He represents something I'm seeing more often lately: men who won't lead. Who defer every decision, who fear direction, who lean on me to be the steady one. And I'm so tired of being the structure. Of being the planner, the emotional anchor, the one always creating the container. I need to be met. Not managed. Not avoided. Not tiptoed around. Met.

And this is what I know now:

I desire a masculine presence that leads—not with control, but with confidence. One that sees my chaos not as something to fix, but as something sacred to hold.

I want devotion. I want loyalty. I want emotional safety. I want someone who sees my fullness and doesn't flinch.

These men—Eddie, Ryan, Tyler—they've all taught me something. They've helped me name my standard. And they've helped me reclaim this truth:

I am not here to mother my partners. I am not here to ask to be adored. I am not here to beg for emotional availability.

I am here to be met.

Not in fantasy. Not in fragments. But in *presence*.

And from now on, I will not confuse attention with devotion. I will not confuse potential with partnership. I will not confuse words with embodiment.

This is me, speaking the standard out loud. And I will not shrink it again.

But speaking the standard is only the beginning.

The real work begins in the quiet moments—the in-between spaces where loneliness creeps in, where old patterns whisper, *"Maybe just this once..."*

That's where I had to meet myself again.

Because the truth is, I didn't just have to let go of them—I had to let go of the version of me who kept circling back. Who mistook crumbs for connection. Who stayed too long, hoping things would be different.

And that's what *Outgrowing the Loop* really means.

Outgrowing the Loop

When Emotional Intimacy Isn't Enough

There's a kind of grief that comes with realizing you've outgrown a connection. It's subtle at first—an internal shift, a flicker of discomfort, a growing awareness that the dynamic no longer feeds your spirit the way it once did. That's what I've been feeling with Miles.

Miles and I have history. We met before Eddie—back when I was still dating and learning what I wanted. He was warm, a little flirtatious, emotionally available in a way that felt safe. But I sensed early on that he was looking for something casual, and I wasn't. So we didn't go further, and things went quiet. It wasn't until nearly a year later, when my relationship with Eddie was starting to fracture, that Miles came back into my life. That's when our friendship deepened.

We became each other's emotional support system. He had just gone through a painful discard with Vanessa, a woman he loved, and I was unraveling in my own toxic situation. We bonded over heartbreak, confusion, and the slow unlearning of our own patterns. Miles taught me about attachment theory and we shared and identified with both having and healing anxious attachment. We shared deeply. We were there for each other.

After I left Eddie and over time, I noticed the energy shifting. Our friendship had become increasingly one-sided. Miles talked—often at length—about Vanessa. His obsession with her hadn't waned, and it was becoming exhausting to hold space for a story that never evolved. I was tired of carrying it. I was tired of the same narrative, the same cycles, and the way he leaned on me without truly checking in on *me*.

We voice messaged a lot. That was our primary form of connection. And yet, even in that, I could feel the imbalance. I would respond thoughtfully. I held space. I reflected. But when I sent something heartfelt or vulnerable, sometimes I was met with silence—or a delay that made it clear I'm not a priority.

What was most revealing is the way Miles had come to *rely* on my emotional support without needing to invest in our friendship physically or energetically. He never made me a priority that way. He didn't need to spend time with me to get what he needed. And I allowed that. But then I started to see the cost.

There was love there. There was respect. But there was also emotional labor I didn't sign up for. And just like in romantic relationships, I didn't want to be in friendships where my energy was extracted without being replenished.

I've grieved this, too. The companionship. The familiarity. The presence. But I'm also choosing to honor the truth:

I've outgrown the loop.

I can love someone and still choose space.

I don't need to carry another story that's not mine.

This is what drawing an energetic boundary looks like. Not with anger, not with resentment—but with reverence for my own capacity.

And I deserve to be held, too.

Boundaries cleared the noise.

But it wasn't just about creating space—it was about listening. Deeply. To my own nervous system. To the subtle ache of unmet needs. To the way my body leaned in or recoiled, long before my mind could catch up.

This is where attunement begins.

Not in fixing or performing—but in feeling. In being felt. In learning to recognize when someone meets you... and when they don't.

Attunement

♥

I don't know. Maybe this is the end. Maybe this is the chapter that closes with me finally seeing him for who he is, not who I wanted him to be.

He kept showing me, over and over, that he wasn't attuned to me. That he didn't listen when I said no, that he didn't remember when I'd set a boundary, that he asked again and again for things I'd already told him I can't give.

And it might be that simple.

I couldn't make him less self-focused. I couldn't force him to be more attuned to me. That's not my job. That's not love. That's not partnership.

And for the first time, I think I really saw that. I saw that loving him wasn't enough to make him see me. I saw that no amount of explaining or repeating myself will ever teach him how to *feel me*.

That's something he has to want to learn on his own. Without me teaching it. Without me breaking myself to show him.

Because if he couldn't hold the tenderness of my boundaries, he would never be able to hold the vastness of my love.

I didn't want to walk him to the door that one time. I didn't want to pretend everything was okay. I didn't want to perform sweetness for him when I was left feeling raw and unseen.

"Do I have to?" I asked.

It wasn't cruel. It was honest. It was the truth of what I felt in that moment – that I owed him nothing more than what I had already given.

Because I'm tired of giving more than I receive. I'm tired of carrying all the weight. And in that tiny moment, standing in my doorway, I finally allowed myself to feel that truth.

And so, I sat there, reflecting on what attunement really meant to me. I knew if I let him go, it could open up the possibility of someone more attuned to me in the ways my body and soul craved. Someone who sees me and listens deeply, without me needing to explain or repeat myself.

But I also knew… I loved him.

I can't expect any person to fulfill everything I need. No one can. What I want is willingness. A willingness to grow. A willingness to meet me where I am. To try.

As frustrated as I was, as much as my heart tightened and my mind spun, I heard that he was expressing willingness. Imperfectly, inconsistently at times, yes, but he was willing right then. And that was something.

I couldn't let him go yet.

I didn't know the outcome. I only knew I still loved him. And maybe love isn't about finding someone who checks off every box or fulfills every unmet need. Maybe love is also about being honest with myself – witnessing what is here and what isn't, and asking: Is there enough willingness for this to grow into something deeper, safer, more nourishing for us both?

So I stayed and decided to watch. I kept my heart soft but my boundaries clear, and I watched to see how it would unfold.

Maybe the bravest thing isn't leaving or staying.

Maybe it's allowing things to unfold without forcing a conclusion—trusting that whatever path reveals itself, I will remain rooted in me.

Because real freedom isn't about walking away to prove a point.

It's about knowing you could... and still choosing presence. It's about staying only when your soul stays, too.

That's the freedom I'm learning to hold.

My True Freedom

♥

Returning to Me Again and Again

I'm sitting with the clarity that **he cannot meet me**. That is the agreement I have to make within myself. He cannot meet me. He kept pushing boundaries. He kept violating them. It may not have been his *intention*, as he said, but it still violated my boundaries.

Earlier, I came across a question for reflection:

"What is your soul no longer willing to tolerate?"

If I've learned anything from the past seven or eight months in Al-Anon, it's this: **The only thing I can control is how I take care of myself and how I uphold my boundaries as standards for MYSELF.**

He couldn't meet me with the love or respect I deserved. His first instinct was always to defend himself—never to pause, listen, or acknowledge the pain I was naming. My feelings were dismissed before they could land. There was no space, no tenderness, no willingness to truly see me. And my soul cannot thrive in that kind of disconnect.

I could feel it in my body. The sick feeling in my stomach had lingered for days. I urged myself to be kind to myself, to be the happy loving woman with myself right in that moment, to hold myself in gentleness and compassion for being human. For being kind of fucked up, you know – knowing I create the chaos and also craving peace in such a deep way.

I revisited Eddie. And in doing so, I reaffirmed a deeper knowing—one that must guide me now, keep me grounded, and help me stay the course. I gave myself permission to return. And now, I must give myself permission to leave again. Just leave. Just let go. Because he kept showing me: my body doesn't trust him. I tense. I brace. There's a familiar knot in my belly. With him, there's always been this undercurrent of self-doubt—like my intuition has been whispering all along. And this time, I have to listen.

He sent words that didn't land in my body. They trigger old wounds—like when he said he missed the intimate imagery we created together. The very thing that made me feel violated and used. Instead of feeling desired, I felt turned off. My stomach had been upset all day.

I knew it's time to let him go.

And maybe I didn't need to announce it. Maybe I just do it in silence.

Because this didn't serve me anymore. It was too hard. It wasn't good for my body. **And my body always knows.**

My nervous system felt agitated—restless, tight, on edge. It wasn't heartbreak anymore. It was irritation. Annoyance. Like an inner voice rising from deep within saying, *Enough*. Stop making space for someone who keeps showing you they don't know how to hold it. Stop giving him access to your softness when he's proven he can't meet it with care. It's not about punishment. It's about protection. My body is wiser now. She's not aching for him—she's warning me. Every time I think of giving him another chance, it's like my whole system recoils: *Please don't put us through that again.* And this time, I'm listening.

And the truth is, I glow up when I'm not dealing with him. When I'm not navigating these frequent mishaps of "oops, he was just riding an emotion," or "oops, he just felt good in the moment so he said it." No. The truth is: **the guy cannot respect boundaries. He cannot take accountability for harm that his behaviour and choices caused.**

I am the invitation. I am the boundary.

Both.

I was sitting outside in my backyard. No phone, no screens. Completely digitally disconnected and more connected to myself than ever. The birdsong was like natural ASMR in the backyard. Breathing, listening, sitting in stillness, in peace. Music playing in the distance from the neighbour's yard.

The past two days, I felt that pit in my stomach again. I learned to adjust to it, but I really craved ease and openness in that area.

I stayed silent with him. Acknowledged his soft breadcrumb. Matched its energy. No more than that. No more over-giving. I've done that before.

I was still angry that my choice – my informed decision-making – was influenced by his deception. It gave me that ick feeling in my belly. I still loved him. Yes. And he gave me an ick feeling. Such a weird place to be.

He commented on my post celebrating my book sales. I hearted it. It was sweet. I mirrored it back, saying "*Thanks babe.*" But I also knew that didn't mean I had to see him or allow him any more access than what he already had.

If he pushed to see me, I would say:

I would need some kind of repair. I can't move closer without it. My body is speaking too loudly.

I've been realizing how **sacred** access really is to me.

Lies give me the ick. Lying erodes trust. I've learned how highly I value honesty and vulnerability in a relationship.

I crave interdependency like the two huge maple trees in my backyard side by side growing, strong, stable. Like the flowers and the bees. Like dark chocolate and peanut butter.

And so, I wrote this letter to release the icky feeling in my stomach:

Letter to Release (A letter you write and never send)

Today I'm writing this letter to release what my heart is holding. In the past few days, you said you missed our intimate imagery. I felt triggered by that again. Like my heart sunk into my belly.

Of course you miss it. It benefited you. But for me, it represents so much pain. It reminded me of the disrespect, of how you violated my trust, my vulnerability, our connection. That ick feeling in my gut remains, two days later.

The recording of our intimacy made me feel used, consumed, objectified, and not enough. When I found out you not only lied, but continued to use other porn and intimate imagery despite all I had shared with you... It brings tears to my eyes again. A lump in my throat. Suddenly, I'm not hungry anymore.

What I long for is deep presence, emotional attunement, tenderness with me – the fullness of me. I need a partner who can take accountability for how their past behaviour, choices, and carelessness with words hurts me and triggers pain all over again.

I release these words from my heart. I do not need you to respond or fix them. I honor my own knowing and choose to come back to myself.

May I trust myself fully. May I choose peace. May I remember my worth.

This is How I End It

I realize now that the screaming goodbye wasn't the true ending. I revisited him, thinking maybe we could repair what was broken. Maybe there was still love strong enough to anchor us through the wreckage.

But the truth is, I didn't go back to him for love. I went back for clarity. I went back to test what my soul was trying to tell me months ago – that he lacks the capacity to truly meet me. Not because he doesn't want to, but because he simply cannot.

Every conversation these past weeks revealed the same pattern. The defensiveness. The dismissiveness. The minimization. I kept hoping he would finally understand my pain, hold it with me, and say *"I see you. I am so sorry. I will do better."* But instead, he responded with confusion and deflection, unable to meet my depth, unable to attune to the tenderness I carry.

I tried to forgive. To soothe. To fix it all. But love isn't built on betrayal, and desire can't thrive under deception. In the end, leaving wasn't just about him. It was about me finally choosing myself.

There's something I don't think I've ever fully said—not even in the earlier reflections of this chapter. I shared more of myself with him than I had with any partner. Not just emotionally, but creatively, intimately. I trusted him with the kind of content I created for my work—content that was deeply personal, sacred, and mine. Most of it was solo, most of it wasn't made *for* him—but I gave him access. I gave him access because I believed we had an agreement of honesty and trust. Because he told me he didn't engage with porn, and that meant something to me. It shaped how safe I felt to share.

But the betrayal wasn't just that he lied. It was that I made decisions based on that lie. I gave him things—parts of me—that I wouldn't have otherwise. And that's the part that haunts me. I wasn't just betrayed. I was manipulated into a false sense of intimacy.

I had already been in silence, trying to let that be the closure. I had said what needed to be said, I had held my boundary. But in the final moments, something else rose up.

When I asked him to delete those videos and photos—the ones he had recorded or that I had shared—I was reclaiming my body, my voice, my *right* to choose who holds that energy. His reaction—dismissive, cruel, sarcastic—told me everything I needed to know.

It wasn't just a betrayal of trust. It was a violation of my consent in retrospect. And when he responded with that final attack on my worth, it cut deeply—but it also gave me clarity. Not just about him, but about what I will never tolerate again.

He lashed out with words that stunned me—not just for their vulgarity, but for their attempt to reduce me to something less than whole. To degrade me down to a single dimension. It was cruel. It was vile. And it landed like a punch to the gut.

I responded. I spoke up—not to win, not to argue, but to reclaim my right to be spoken to with respect. Maybe I should've stayed quiet. I had been practicing that. But something in me knew I needed to stand tall in that moment. Not for him. For me.

Because those words? They weren't mine to carry.

They were projections. A reflection of his own pain, his limitations, his jealousy. I represented everything he couldn't meet in himself, let alone in me.

Later, I sat with it all—the shame, the ache, the confusion. I asked myself the hard questions: *How could I have spent two years with this man? Was this always there under the surface, waiting to erupt? Should I have stayed silent?*

But the truth was, I didn't need more analysis. I didn't need to unravel it further. Those final words gave me something else: clarity.

And in that clarity, I knew—it was over. Completely.

I blocked him everywhere: phone, social media, even mutual contacts. And I felt it... the final emotional and energetic tether snap. The pain was deep, but the cut was clean.

And in that severing, I found something I had been searching for all along:

True freedom.

I get to choose myself over and over again. That's my lesson, and maybe yours is something along those lines too.

And as I sit here with the ache in my belly finally softening, I realize:

I didn't go back because I was weak. I went back because I needed to know for certain that my soul was right. I needed to see, one more time, that peace does not live in his presence. I needed to feel it so deeply in my body that I could no longer ignore it.

I forgive myself for reopening old wounds. I forgive myself for hoping he could be more than he is. I forgive myself for loving him with all of me, even when he could not love me in the way I needed.

Even when I revisit things out of clarity or for my own healing process, it's okay. Because I always have the option to return to myself at any time.

That is my true freedom.

I realized I had been waiting around for an ending to this memoir. I even said it out loud to Eddie – *I haven't been able to write the ending because you're part of it.*

But then it hit me: **the ending starts with me. Choosing myself is the ending and the beginning.**

I choose the ending. I choose myself, again and again. I choose peace over chaos. I choose my glow over this ache. I choose a life that nourishes my nervous system. I choose a love that feels like ease in my body. I hold the line and let fall away what falls away. I let the cards fall. I let go and let God.

Maybe that's the real lesson: To *always* focus back on me. To choose me, every time.

Maybe this is the final time. The time I walk away and break the cycle. This time, I don't walk right back into the same dynamic with a different person. This time, I break the pattern.

He was never meant to be my forever. He was a lesson in knowing what I can no longer tolerate. He was a mirror, a test, a karmic ache, but not my home.

And it's okay.

This is the ending.

I am the ending. And the beginning. So are you. I decide. I choose. So do you.

Because I am my own home. And I am walking myself back there, again and again, until I finally remember:

I never left.

I was the one I was waiting for all along.

Letter to the Reader

♥

This isn't just my story. It's the story of every woman who has ever silenced herself to be loved, every mother who has risen from the ashes, every heart who has shattered only to find its truth in the fragments.

May these words remind you: Your worth – it's not negotiable. Your voice is not too much. Your love is not a burden. You are the home you have been waiting for.

Heather Wild

xo

A Note to Readers

If this book moved you, resonated with you, or made you feel less alone in your own journey—I would be deeply grateful if you left a review. Your words help others find this story, and they mean more than you know.

Leave a review on Amazon or Goodreads and let others know what this book awakened in you.

Stay Connected

Sacred Anchors for the Moments You Want to Reach Out

I've created 8 phone wallpapers as quiet reminders—sacred anchors for the moments when you're tempted to check, reach, or ruminate. These affirmations are meant to live on your lock screen, offering pause, power, and perspective exactly when you need it most.

https://www.heateronhealth.com/pages/sacred-quote-collection-free-download

***

This memoir is just the beginning of the conversation. I share more writing, embodiment practices, and behind-the-scenes reflections across platforms. Come say hello:

Instagram: https://www.instagram.com/heather.conscious-woman

Website: https://www.heateronhealth.com

YouTube: Heather Wild's Sensual Flow Academy

I WAS THE ONE I WAS WAITING FOR

About the Author

Heather Wild is a writer, embodiment guide, and mother who weaves sensuality, spirituality, and raw human truth into every facet of her work. With a background spanning nursing, mental health, yoga, and feminine embodiment, she holds space for others to reclaim their worth, remember their wholeness, and rewrite their stories.

Heather is passionate about helping women come home to their bodies through sensual movement, mindful self-expression, and radical self-love. Her writing explores themes of love, loss, attachment, healing, and the sacred reclamation of the feminine self.

She lives in Ontario, Canada, raising her children with the same fierce tenderness and wild honesty she brings to her words. When she isn't writing or guiding others through embodiment practices, you can find her dancing barefoot in her living room, whispering prayers to the trees, or curled up with a cup of coffee and her journal.

I Was the One I Was Waiting For is her first memoir. She hopes these pages remind readers of their own worth and guide them back to the truth they've always carried within:

You are the one you've been waiting for.

www.ingramcontent.com/pod-product-compliance
Lightning Source LLC
Chambersburg PA
CBHW071252070526

44583CB00017B/2430